D0629715

Promises from God for

Single
Women

PROMISES FROM GOD FOR

Single Women

T. D. JAKES

BERKLEY BOOKS, NEW YORK

THE BERKLEY PUBLISHING GROUP
Published by the Penguin Group
Penguin Group (USA) Inc.
375 Hudson Street, New York, New York 10014, USA
Penguin Group (Canada), 90 Eglinton Avenue East, Suite 700, Toronto, Ontario M4P 2Y3, Canada
(a division of Pearson Penguin Canada Inc.)
Penguin Books Ltd., 80 Strand, London WC2R 0RL, England
Penguin Group Ireland, 25 St. Stephen's Green, Dublin 2, Ireland (a division of Penguin Books Ltd.)
Penguin Group (Australia), 250 Camberwell Road, Camberwell, Victoria 3124, Australia
(a division of Pearson Australia Group Pty. Ltd.)
Penguin Books India Pvt. Ltd., 11 Community Centre, Panchsheel Park, New Delhi—110 017, India
Penguin Group (NZ), Cnr. Airborne and Rosedale Roads, Albany, Auckland 1310, New Zealand
(a division of Pearson New Zealand Ltd.)
Penguin Books (South Africa) (Pty.) Ltd., 24 Sturdee Avenue, Rosebank, Johannesburg 2196,
South Africa

Penguin Books Ltd., Registered Offices: 80 Strand, London WC2R 0RL, England

PROMISES FROM GOD FOR SINGLE WOMEN

This book is an original publication of The Berkley Publishing Group.

First edition: August 2005

Berkley hardcover ISBN: 978-0-425-20662-1

This book has been catalogued with the Library of Congress.

PRINTED IN THE UNITED STATES OF AMERICA

20   19   18   17   16   15   14   13   12   11

I would like to dedicate this book to my sister, Jacqueline Jakes. She is a writer in her own right—a single woman whose amazing faith has impressed me and whose wisdom has often caused my spirit to soar to heights unknown. Thanks for sharing your wisdom to the world, offering practical solutions to singles, and powerful truths to all who love Jesus as much as we do! You sang to me when I was young and pray for me now that I am not. When life is hard, I hear your singing in my soul. When I need encouragement, I often read your words and weep. Keep writing to our souls.

CONTENTS

INTRODUCTION

I remember sitting in a restaurant not too long ago. I was having a business lunch and my dining companion called to say he was running late. I occupied myself by perusing the menu, but after looking over the dessert options for the third time, I closed the menu and scanned the dining room, thinking that people-watching would prove more entertaining. There was the usual business crowd—men and women dressed in suits discussing mergers, acquisitions, and the latest market trends. A few tables were filled with obviously well-dressed women, often called "ladies who lunch," talking about upcoming charity events and socialite gossip. But the table that seemed most interesting to me was one nearby occupied by three young women. I didn't mean to eavesdrop on their conversation, but they were so animated and talking so loudly, that I couldn't help but overhear. They were chatting about an episode of the show *Sex and the City* that had recently re-aired. They were laughing about the dating adventures of the characters on the show, relating to their various problems with men, and lamenting about how difficult it was to be a single woman today.

It wasn't a conversation that was totally unfamiliar to me. Many women in my church have come to me asking for advice on how to deal with the various issues that single women face. But I believe that single Christian women face greater challenges, caught in a society where television, movies, and the latest issue of the popular women's magazines all portray a certain image of the successful, happy single woman, and the church offers a prescription that is often quite contradictory. I imagine that it's easy for a Christian sister to become confused and frustrated, wanting to follow God's Word, eager to find love and a life partner, and tempted by the carnal pleasures that have enticed humans since the time of Adam and Eve in the Garden of Eden. She may be getting pressure from family, friends, and even fellow church members to marry. She may be struggling with finding suitable men to date. And, of course, there is sexual temptation. It's hard for her to stay on the Path when it is often obscured by popular culture and the illusions of our own human frailty.

And it is not just younger women who are facing these issues. Women in their thirties who pursued careers may feel desperation about never finding love as they hear the ticking—or for some, booming—of their biological clocks. Then there are those who are fifty, sixty, and even older who find themselves single later in life and totally lost, questioning how to navigate the dating scene. No, I don't think it's easy.

It is not fair to assume that every singe woman wants to be married. I have known many women who have become comfortable with their singleness. Contrary to what some teach on this subject, singleness is not a disease. It is a sign of wholeness. To be single is what one is when he or she is not fractioned. It can be an indication of wholeness. If one is not whole before marriage I must warn that marriage will not complete a broken soul.

Although I know many single women who are leading lives that are full and fulfilled, one of the most common issues that is often brought to me is how difficult it is to find a "good man." I hear complaints about how men are "only after one thing," or only want women who look like fashion models (even though they themselves might be far from *GQ* material). And worst of all are the stories of betrayal and infidelity. I hear too many tearful accounts of cheating boyfriends, broken promises, and women feeling played by someone they loved and trusted.

But what's astonishing to me is that after they relate these sad tales, women usually end the saga with the plea "Bishop, tell me what's wrong with me!" as if they are responsible for the bad behavior they've been subjected to. They worry that they are not pretty enough, thin enough, smart enough, sexy enough . . . just not enough. They vow to work harder, dress more fashionably, and find a way to win back this man they just called a dog! And all of a sudden it becomes all about what they lack and what they need to do to become "more of a woman."

At the same time, a curious thing happens. Their anger

and disdain get redirected to other women whom they view as their "competition." Catty comments and jealous judgments about who wears her skirts too short and blouses cut too low. Ugly rumors about who did what to get a man. Scheming plans to "get back my man from that witch who stole him away." These ladies get caught up trying to learn the rules, break the code, and win the game.

Sister, does this scenario sound familiar to you? Do you see your girlfriends, or yourself, in the description above? Well, I want to offer you a reality check. I want to share with you some observations from the many years my wife and I have ministered to single women. More important, I want to lead you to God's Word, which reassures you that you are more than enough and everything He created you to be. You are a daughter of God and He created you to complete and utter perfection. You are part of His perfect plan, right now, right as you are. Not when you lose weight, not when you find a boyfriend, not when you get married. Right now!

Although you may sometimes feel lonely, remember that you are never alone. Our Father walks beside you and will never abandon you. Don't let desperation lead you to destruction. It is so easy to get swept up in the soap opera–like entanglements of this world, but set your sights on fulfilling the purpose God has set before you. He has a plan for you and it will happen in His time in His way—not one minute before.

Gather Your Oil

As a Christian woman, you have more important things to do than obsess about finding a mate. Don't worry. Know that God has someone or something waiting for you. Your only job is to fulfill God's purpose for you. You need to walk the path He has laid before you, serve Him and only Him, and prepare yourself for all He has in store for you. Becoming too caught up in the dating/mating/relating game distracts you from your Heavenly calling and keeps you from the Lord.

It reminds me of the parable of the wise and foolish virgins (Matthew 25:1–13). There were ten virgins who took their lamps and went to meet the bridegroom. The wise virgins filled their lamps with oil and took it with them, but the foolish ones left without any oil. They were probably so excited and so worried about making a good impression that they failed to prepare themselves for the meeting.

> And at midnight a cry was heard, "Behold, the bridegroom is coming; go out to meet him!" Then all those virgins arose and trimmed their lamps. And the foolish said to the wise, "Give us some of your oil, for our lamps are going out." But the wise answered saying, "No, lest there should not be enough for us and you; but go rather to those who sell, and buy for yourselves." And while they went to buy, the bridegroom came, and those who were ready went in with him to the wedding; and the door was shut."
>
> (MATTHEW 25: 1–10)

This parable speaks of Jesus the Bridegroom, and it instructs us to prepare ourselves to meet Him because we never know when He may come. Ladies, don't be so busy primping and fussing and worrying about where you're going to go on Saturday night, that you get left out in the darkness and miss seeing the Light! Don't be so caught up in the concerns of this world that you forget to gather your oil! Be mindful of the Lord, read His Word, attend to His service, and ready yourself for His coming. Do your part and He will take care of you. He will attend to every one of your needs. Walk with God and he will lead you to your destiny.

God Keeps His Promises

I know that sometimes it may be difficult to just "let go and let God." Another broken heart, another betrayal, or another weekend alone—how can you not feel despair and loneliness? I'll tell you how. You have to have faith. God has promised to give you the desires of your heart (Delight yourself also in the Lord, And He shall give you the desires of your heart.—Psalms 37:4). And God never breaks His promises. He will reward those who seek Him. He may not come when you want Him to, but He'll come just on time. If you wait on the Lord, He'll come through.

But you have to do your part. Your part is to keep faith. Just because you can't see it now, doesn't mean God won't do it. Just because something doesn't seem possible doesn't mean it will never happen. All things are possible through God, and He will make all things possible for you.

Remember Sarah. She had faith that she could conceive a child even though she was well beyond childbearing age. It was biologically impossible for her to birth a child at her age. It went against the laws of nature. But Sarah had faith and God kept His promise. And what about Abraham? He received many promises from God regarding his descendents, and through the darkest times he still believed that God would keep His covenant. And God did.

It's in those darkest times that we need to make sure we have our oil. Throughout the Bible, oil is used to represent the Holy Spirit. The Holy Spirit can shine a light and break through the darkness. The Holy Spirit can lead us out of our despair. Yes, we must keep our faith and we must keep God within us. The only thing that God asks of us is that we keep faith in Him. We must keep our promise to Him, and he will fulfill all His promises to us.

Throughout these pages, you will find some of God's promises to you. When you are troubled, look to His Word and be heartened. When you are in darkness, find comfort in His Light. I have chosen twelve topics that I've seen touch single women the most, but if you don't see a specific subject that you're looking for, just dive in—God's Word covers everything.

At the end of this little book, you will find Promise Pages. It is here that you should remind yourself of the promises God has made you and the promises He has fulfilled. Remember that God is the Promise Keeper.

God promises you so much. Don't you think you should make promises to Him in return? You will also find pages where you can record your promises to the Lord. Exchange vows with the Lord. Let God be your Spiritual Husband. He will be by your side in good times and in bad, in sickness and in health, for richer or for poorer. You may be a single woman, but you are never alone. Wherever you are, God is with you.

Loneliness

Loneliness

And you cannot be my disciple if you do not
carry your own cross and follow me. But don't
begin until you count the cost.

(Luke 14:27–28a*)

Loneliness can feel so heavy, like carrying a huge cross on your back. Over and over in the Bible we are told that there is a reason and purpose for everything that we have to endure in our lives. There are times when I have felt the weight of something heavy in my life and couldn't see the purpose . . . until days or months or even years later. And then I was able to see how that experience was used to shape me into a stronger follower of Christ. Have heart and know that the heaviness will not last forever, that Jesus has promised to carry your burden, and that by surrendering to God, we are living on the path of the righteous.

YOUR PROMISE TO GOD . . .

Lord, I am lonely, and I cannot see Your will. Please guide me, help me, show me Your way. I'm ready to listen now.

Loneliness

If we endure hardship, we will reign with him.

(II Timothy 2:12a*)

I don't know the hardships you have faced, and I cannot pretend to be able to heal them for you. However, I do know about hardship and pain, and I've met many women who have shared their hardships and pain with me. Though our situations might be individualized, there is a solution that is generalized: prayer. God promises throughout the holy Bible that by praying earnestly and humbly we will be shown the way. God promises that by following His Word, we can begin to experience joy. God promises that living in His kingdom will lead to everlasting life. Hardships are a temporary experience, though they sometimes feel eternal. The only eternal experience is the True Experience of Christ Jesus.

YOUR PROMISE TO GOD . . .

In times of hardship and struggle, I will lift up my voice to You. I will pray for Your blessings and find peace in Your arms.

Loneliness

But remember that the temptations that come into your life are no different from what others experience. And God is faithful. He will keep the temptation from becoming so strong that you can't stand up against it. When you are tempted, he will show you a way out so that you will not give in to it.

(1 Corinthians 10:13*)

Here is a simple truth to remember: when you say no to something, you are really saying yes to something else. Saying no to worldly activities or sexual temptations might make you feel lonely in the short term, but what you are actually doing is saying yes to the Godly life, yes to reaching out and touching the hem of Christ Himself. When you say no to activities that will keep you bound in the prison of sin, you are saying yes to being set free into the kingdom of God. Ask God to help you develop discernment so that you will know what to say no to, and what you are really saying yes to.

YOUR PROMISE TO GOD . . .

Yes, God, yes! I say no to the world, and yes to You!

Loneliness

God blesses the people who patiently endure test-
ing. Afterward they will receive the crown of life
that God has promised to those who love him.

(James 1:12 *)

Patience is a virtue, we're told, but it's hard to be patient when loneliness grabs hold of our heart and it seems like it won't let go. But what will break the key grip of loneliness is a faithful heart that understands that God's promises are more real than the world's lies. Don't fret, sister, and don't let the devil bring you down. Be lifted up into the truth of the Lord.

YOUR PROMISE TO GOD . . .

I know You will lift the loneliness from my heart. I will wait faithfully until Your time.

Loneliness

In his kindness God called you to his eternal glory by means of Jesus Christ. After you have suffered a little while, he will restore, support, and strengthen you, and he will place you on a firm foundation.

(1 Peter 5:10*)

How in love with Jesus are you? How firm of a foundation have you built with your Lord? How often do you call Him, seek Him, talk to Him, pray to Him, read His word, and bask in His glory? You see, God has called you specifically—and even though you cannot see Him, He sees you. He sees the authentic you that you may not even see in yourself; the greater you that He made for His purpose. By looking to Him at every turn, you will be allowing Him to place in you and your life a foundation on which He can do amazing things. Answer His call now.

YOUR PROMISE TO GOD . . .

God, I will seek You out and call Your name at every turn. I love You with all my heart.

Loneliness

Don't be troubled. You trust God, now trust in me.

(John 14:1*)

What does trusting in Jesus entail from you? If you are feeling lonely, how does this Bible verse apply to your life? I don't know your specific situation, but what I can tell you is that trusting in Jesus is the one answer that will make a permanent change in your life. You've probably already tried every other method you can think of—alcohol, drugs, sex, overspending, overeating, undereating, and on and on—and none of those has taken away the loneliness. Perhaps you are surrounded by people or even are in a relationship and still feel lonely. Why? Because peace of mind comes from trust in the Lord. Trust means to surrender without hesitation, knowing that God will come through for you. Trusting means opening up and allowing Jesus to move in and do some miraculous work in your life.

YOUR PROMISE TO GOD . . .

Lord, I trust You to take away my loneliness. You, and You alone, can transform my life, and I am ready for Your blessing.

Friendship

Friendship

He cuts off every branch that doesn't produce
fruit, and he prunes the branches that do bear
fruit so they will produce even more.

(John 15:2*)

Do something for me—go get your address book and a black marker. Across the front write the words "By Invitation Only." Now go through the book, page by page, person by person, and evaluate if each relationship is one that bears fruit or not. It is important to put your time and energy into those relationships that raise you up and glorify the Lord.

YOUR PROMISE TO GOD . . .

I don't have time for people who keep me down. I will only invest myself in relationships that bring me closer to You.

Friendship

If people persecute you because you are a Christ-ian, don't curse them; pray that God will bless them. When others are happy, be happy with them. If they are sad, share their sorrow. Live in harmony with each other. Don't try to act impor-tant, but enjoy the company of ordinary people. And don't think you know it all!

(Romans 12:14–16*)

You see Miss So-and-So get a new boyfriend, and you're jealous. Or you see Mrs. Across-the-Street get a new car, and you feel like you deserve one more than she does. And who does she think she is anyway?

Woman, those kind of thoughts are dangerous! They build walls between you and others. Banish them from your thinking and replace them with thoughts of compassion and generosity. Ask God each morning, "Who do you want me to help today?" God will bring into your path people who need exactly the encouragement and help that you can give them. (And by the way, that person who needs encouragement and help might be yourself—being a friend to yourself is an important relationship to foster!)

YOUR PROMISE TO GOD . . .

I will encourage—not envy—others. You give me all I need so that I can share myself with those who need me.

Friendship

So don't condemn each other anymore. Decide instead to live in such a way that you will not put an obstacle in another Christian's path.

(Romans 14:13*)

Being a powerful woman of God comes with its own responsibilities. It is not enough to avoid some sinful behavior. No! To be a true shining example of the power of Christ to change your life, you must actively not do anything that might be a stumbling block to other Christians. Jesus Himself told us to be in the world, but do not be of it. What does that mean for you? Pray about it, and ask God to show you where you might be slipping, where you might be falling down on your responsibilities. Listen and watch—you will be given a burden in your heart to stop certain activities or behaviors. Know that this is God's will, and He is preparing you for greater glory by paring down what keeps you small.

YOUR PROMISE TO GOD . . .

I want to be the kind of friend who uplifts and upholds God's glory. Show me what I need to do and I will follow Your counsel.

Friendship

May God, who gives this patience and encouragement, help you live in complete harmony with each other—each with the attitude of Christ Jesus toward the other.

(Romans 15:5*)

Your girlfriend is getting on your nerves big-time! What do you do? Do you call up another girlfriend and complain? Do you hold resentment and anger and let it well up inside you? Let me give you a piece of advice: turn to the Lord. Read His Word. Walk in the footsteps of Christ Jesus and learn His way. Focus on God to give you patience. Pray to God to heal any rift you might have, and pray that God brings joy to your girlfriend. Isn't that what you want her to do for you? You do it first. Be the example!

YOUR PROMISE TO GOD . . .

As a daughter of God, I want to get along with all my sisters. I will be patient, understanding, and supportive.

Friendship

I command you to love each other in the same way that I love you.

(John 15:12 *)

Let me tell you a story about these two women who were good friends. They decided to bring God into their friendship and began studying the Bible together once a week. They found their friendship deepening, strengthening, and are now committed Prayer Partners. They are changing the world through their friendship. As the Lord said, "Wherever two or more are gathered in My name . . ."

YOUR PROMISE TO GOD . . .

Two is company, but three is never a crowd when God is with me. In fact, the more the merrier. I will make God the foundation of all my friendships and my friendships will thrive because of it.

Friendship

There are "friends" who destroy each other, but a real friend sticks closer than a brother.

(*Proverbs 18:24**)

True friends are like precious diamonds—they shine brightly when you hold them up to the light, and are more valuable every year you have them. Take good care of those very special people in your life. God has sent them to you to take special care of you. Celebrate them as the gifts they are and never take them for granted.

Your Promise to God . . .

My friends are like precious jewels. I will treasure them forever.

Betrayal

Betrayal

Watch out for anyone who tells lies and flatters—they are out to get you.
(Proverbs 26:28[†])

You thought he was Mr. Looks-So-Good, but in reality he was just Mr. Looks-So-Gone. Give him up! Let him go! Yes, he hurt you. Yes, he'll keep hurting you as long as you hold on to the hurt. Clean up this relationship, walk away with your head held high. Know that you are praising the Lord for taking you out of a relationship that did not honor you and, in fact, defiled your spirit. Don't turn back—stay strong! Letting go not only makes you feel brand-new again, but it also clears the way for God to bring you Mr. Right. Why settle for table scraps when God will bring you His bounty!

YOUR PROMISE TO GOD . . .

Lord, it may hurt to say goodbye, but I know You're preparing me to say hello to my future.

Betrayal

Those who lead the upright into sin will fall into
their own trap, but the honest will inherit good
things.

(Proverbs 28:10*)

Your "friend" has done you wrong. Shame on her. But let's be clear about one thing—her behavior is her business. She may have hurt you, but don't let her have enough power in your life to stop you dead in your tracks. Forgive her, as hard as that may be, and then put on your boots and start walking. You don't need "friends" like that in your life. Be an example of letting go and letting God handle the matter. He will, and He will always take care of you, too.

YOUR PROMISE TO GOD . . .

Friends who hurt me are no friends of mine. I will sweep out the trash and trust that You are my best friend, sure and true.

Betrayal

Do not fret because of evildoers, nor be envious of the wicked; for there will be no prospect for the evil man; the lamp of the wicked will be put out.

(Proverbs 24:19–20)

Girl, pay attention to your own life. You've got too much going on to worry about what he-said/she-said. Wasting time on all that trash is wasting your treasure. Betrayal by a friend can hurt; it can sting like the bite of a scorpion. But God will never betray you. Keep your focus on Him and watch those scorpions slither out of your life.

Your Promise to God . . .

I will focus my gaze on Jesus and let betrayers stay out of my sight. Jesus is all I need.

Betrayal

The mouths of fools are their ruin; their lips get them into trouble. What dainty morsels rumors are—but they sink deep into one's heart.

(Proverbs 18:7–8*)

That delicious piece of gossip seems so sweet. But betraying another person, whether friend or foe, makes our life sour. God abhors gossip, and for good reason: Betraying another can only bear the fruit of pain and suffering. Is that how God would have you act? Think twice—and then think again—before speaking or acting against another, no matter who they are.

YOUR PROMISE TO GOD . . .

Talking trash hurts others, myself, and God. I will only let sweetness come out of my mouth.

Betrayal

My dear brothers and sisters, be quick to listen,
slow to speak, and slow to get angry. Your anger
can never make things right in God's sight.

(James 1:19–20*)

Trying to keep up with everyone who has done you wrong is a can't-win game. Spending time and energy trying to deal with who hurt you first and who hurt you most is never-ending. God does not want you to waste even one more precious moment dealing in the level of other people's smallness. God has a great destiny for you. So let it go, girl, and get on with it.

YOUR PROMISE TO GOD . . .

Does it really matter who hurt me when God is here to heal me? I will let go and let God bring greatness into my life.

Betrayal

I will sing of the tender mercies of the Lord forever!
Young and old will hear of your faithfulness.
Your unfailing love will last forever. Your faithful-
ness is as enduring as the heavens.

(Psalm 89:1–2*)

Let me make one thing clear, m'lady—while people can betray you, God never will. You are His lady and He loves you perfectly. It's sometimes difficult to fathom how precious He holds you in His sight, but do not ever doubt it. When you feel betrayed by situations and persons you encounter, immediately come back to the great truth—God is faithful. Be faithful to Him!

YOUR PROMISE TO GOD . . .

God, I will be faithful to You for You are eternally faithful to me. I am your lady! I rejoice!

Forgiveness

Forgiveness

And whenever you stand praying, if you have anything against anyone, forgive him, that your Father in heaven may also forgive you your trespasses.

(Mark 11:25)

He may have done you wrong—lies, cheating, trampling on your heart. But don't let bitterness and anger consume you. Holding on to the hurt and blame will only stop the flow of God's love in your life. Let it go! Forgive him but then continue on your journey toward the fullness that awaits you.

YOUR PROMISE TO GOD . . .

I don't need to take any excess baggage on my trip to destiny. I'm going to let that hurt go and carry on my way.

Forgiveness

Forgive us our sins, just as we have forgiven those
who have sinned against us. If you forgive those
who sin against you, your heavenly Father will
forgive you. But if you refuse to forgive others,
your Father will not forgive your sins.

(Matthew 6:12, 14–15*)

Holding on to unforgiveness is like holding on to a serpent—it will keep biting you and inflicting you with its poison until you let it go. Girl, drop that vile serpent of blame before your life becomes toxic from the venom. Forgiveness will cleanse your life like great medicine from God. Make a list and begin forgiving others (and yourself) starting today. God promises to forgive you once you come clean with those who you have yet to forgive.

YOUR PROMISE TO GOD . . .

I will follow Jesus' example and forgive those who have done me wrong.

Forgiveness

Let all bitterness, wrath, anger, clamor, and evil speaking be put away from you, with all malice. And be kind to one another, tenderhearted, forgiving one another, even as God in Christ forgave you.

(Ephesians 4:31–32)

When we withhold forgiveness from another, it can cause us to engage in unseemly behavior. I'm talking to you! You know that playing the blame game will yield only losers, no winners. Here's the best game in town—forgiving others actually frees you! It allows you to live lighter and see more clearly. And it opens the way for God to forgive you and cleanse your heart. This is the true game of life—play it now and win!

YOUR PROMISE TO GOD . . .

I am going on a no-blame diet. I will forgive others and lighten my soul.

Forgiveness

An angry person is dangerous, but a jealous person is even worse.

(Proverbs 27:4[+])

Have you ever been the subject of someone else's jealousy? It doesn't feel good. It feels like an attack on your spirit. If feels unjustified and unwarranted. And you might even feel the need for revenge. Woman, lay down the weapons in your mind and take up the soothing peace of your soul. God is present here, and will not forsake you, though someone else did. God is the great corrector of all situations, and will bring justice about in His time, not in yours. How the situation resolves itself is none of your business! But what is your business is how you resolve things in your own mind. Let go of their behavior, let go of their petty jealousy, and stay standing in the light of God. Stay in the firm conviction of the heart. Return their bile with God's roses.

YOUR PROMISE TO GOD . . .

I have no time for jealousy in my life. You will take care of all of this nonsense. And I know that You will take care of me.

Forgiveness

If you don't confess your sins, you will be a fail-ure. But God will be merciful if you confess your sins and give them up.

(Proverbs 28:13†)

You might have a past filled with events or people you'd rather forget. You might have been wronged or done wrong—either way, you've got baggage. Don't let shame or blame keep you from receiving the sweet gift of God's forgiveness. Hand over the baggage of sin and sinful behavior to the Lord, and He promises your burden will be forever light. God loves you despite your past—now it is time for you to bask in the glow of forgiving others and forgiving yourself.

Your Promise to God . . .

No matter what I've done or where I've been, I know You have a one-way ticket for me to glory. You have obliterated the road behind me and I will follow the great, new one You have set before me.

Forgiveness

And he [the Prodigal Son] arose and came to his father. But when he was still a great way off, his father saw him and had compassion, and ran and fell on his neck and kissed him.

(Luke 15:20)

Are you a Prodigal Daughter? Jesus teaches us in this story that our willingness to humble ourselves before the Lord and return back to Him will be met with great compassion and love. What have you been withholding from God? Run—don't walk—back to God the Father with a humbled heart, and go from Prodigal Daughter to Victorious Daughter of God.

YOUR PROMISE TO GOD . . .

I may have stumbled along the way, but now I'm running to You with my arms wide open ready to be embraced by my Father.

Sex

Sex

To the pure all things are pure; but to those who are defiled and unbelieving nothing is pure; but even their mind and conscience are defiled.

(Titus 1:15)

Yes, he's handsome. Yes, your body yearns. And yes, if you succumb to temptation, you might experience a temporary feeling like you have won his heart. But it's a hollow victory, because you have just lost God's heart. God is very clear: do not have sexual relations outside of the sanctity of marriage. Period. If you defy God today, where will that leave you tomorrow? Entreat God to help make you strong, and if that man can't wait until what God has ordained, he just isn't the man God has in store for you. Wait for quality, rather than settle for quantity.

YOUR PROMISE TO GOD . . .

I am a beautiful flower in the Lord's garden and I won't let anyone spoil my beauty before the appointed time.

Sex

Do not enter the path of the wicked, and do not walk in the way of evil. Avoid it, do not travel on it; turn away from it and pass on.

(*Proverbs 4:14–15*)

The fruit of the tree is sweet, but the aftertaste of giving in to temptation is bitter indeed. Is one hour of pleasure worth a lifetime of pain? Sometimes you may be tempted to succumb to the yearning of the flesh, but the Lord rewards those who yield against the temptation with purity, inner peace, and that true, sweet knowing that you are walking the path of righteousness. Sister, love yourself more than you love your needs. Love God more than you love sin.

YOUR PROMISE TO GOD . . .

The flesh may be weak, but God in my heart is stronger. I will remain pure and please my Lord.

Sex

For the lips of an immoral woman drip honey, and her mouth is smoother than oil, but in the end she is bitter as wormwood, sharp as a two-edged sword. Her feet go down to death, her steps lay hold of hell. Lest you ponder her path of life—her ways are unstable, you do not know them.

(Proverbs 5:3–6)

You see other women using their sexual wiles to snare a man. Don't stoop to their sinful level. You have a more powerful weapon on your side—Jesus Christ. He wants you to honor yourself and trust in Him to send you Mr. Right rather than Mr. Right Now. The wait will be well worth it.

YOUR PROMISE TO GOD . . .

I don't have to use my body to win a man. You have my heart and I know that You will provide for me.

Sex

For the world offers only the lust for physical pleasure, the lust for everything we see, and pride in our possessions. These are not from the Father. They are from this evil world. And this world is fading away, along with everything it craves. But if you do the will of God, you will live forever.

(1 John 2:16–17*)

It is said that the biggest sexual organ is the brain. But it's hard to remember that when you look around and see that the world is forcing images of the body at you from every angle—from immoral television shows to sinful music lyrics, even to pornographic Internet content. Use that brain to remember something very important, which is that the body is temporary, and the consequences of lust are forever. The repercussions of giving in to temptation will last a lot longer than the sexual act itself. Is it worth it? Stay strong in the Lord. Stay smart in your mind. Stay chaste in your body.

YOUR PROMISE TO GOD . . .

Lord, there are sinful influences all around me, but I will keep You in my heart, and You will protect me from temptation.

Sex

So I advise you to live according to your new life in the Holy Spirit. Then you won't be doing what your sinful nature craves. The old sinful nature loves to do evil, which is just opposite from what the Holy Spirit wants. And the Spirit gives us desires that are opposite from what the sinful nature desires. These two forces are constantly fighting each other, and your choices are never free from this conflict. But when you are directed by the Holy Spirit, you are no longer subject to the law.

(Galatians 5:16–18*)

Here's a secret about long-lasting relationships: the love that a man and a woman share endures if there is a mighty base of friendship. Ultimately, the friendship aspect of a romantic relationship is as intimate as the joining of the flesh. It is a different aspect of the same intimate act of a relationship. But until the actual marriage, it is best to build the friendship foundation that will create the strongest platform for you and your beloved to build upon. Yes, physical attraction is important, but being able to share interests, values, and faith is longer-lasting. God gave sexuality as a gift, and one that is to be enjoyed responsibly. God also gave intimate friendship as a gift, and that is one gift you and your partner can begin to share and expand upon now.

YOUR PROMISE TO GOD . . .

Although the flesh is weak, I will remain strong knowing that a foundation of friendship will make for a stronger relationship and is pleasing to You.

Sex

*But if we confess our sins to God, he can always
be trusted to forgive us and take our sins away.*

(I John 1:9[+])

You slipped. You messed up. You have a checkered past that includes some behavior that you are no longer proud of, and you have a burden in your heart about it. Can God forgive you? Of course! Will God forgive you? That is up to you. As a born-again Christian you became washed clean of your past sins, and even of the past sins that were thrust upon you. Completely made new. Christ took care of your sins on that glorious day of resurrection. Now, to be forgiven of your sins, you must do something that might be hard, and that is to give them up to the Lord. Give Him your sins and tell Him you are sorry. Give Him your past and tell Him you forgive yourself, or you forgive anyone who abused you. Give Him your present-day fears and doubts. And give Him your tomorrow. With God in the lead, you will be led to higher ground.

YOUR PROMISE TO GOD . . .

Dear Jesus, wash me clean of my sins and lead me on the path of righteousness. I give over my past to You so that I may be born anew.

Healing

Healing

For you were once darkness, but now you are light in the Lord. Walk as children of light (for the fruit of the Spirit is in all goodness, righteousness, and truth), finding out what is acceptable to the Lord.

(Ephesians 5:8–10)

It's so easy to walk around feeling like darkness is engulfing you, pain is paralyzing you. But take heart, my friend, for God hears your weeping and will wipe away your tears. No matter how broken you feel, no matter how many pieces your heart has shattered in, know that the Lord wants to lift you up and make you whole. Say yes to this healing power, and live from this moment on in this glory.

YOUR PROMISE TO GOD . . .

In moments of darkness, I will always seek the Light, for I know You are always with me.

Healing

But Jesus turned around, and when He saw her He said: "Be of good cheer daughter; your faith has made you well."

(Matthew 9:22)

You say you believe in the unlimited power of Jesus, but you have doubts. Does He really love you? What's His will for you? Doubt no more! The Lord has promised that the faithful shall be rewarded. Don't despair, for despair is a barrier between you and God. Like the example of the daughter mentioned in Matthew 9:22—by your faith God will set you free.

Your Promise to God . . .

I do believe in the unlimited power of Jesus. No matter how I feel, I will remember that He can lift me up.

Healing

Pay attention, my child, to what I say. Listen carefully. Don't lose sight of my words. Let them penetrate deep within your heart, for they bring life and radiant health to anyone who discovers their meaning.

(Proverbs 4:20–22*)

The Lord is Lord of all of your life. He is not just a Sunday god, or someone who lived a couple of thousand years ago. He is the Lord right here and right now—as you are reading these words—and He is the Lord in every area of your life. And that includes the areas you might want to hide, or that you are ashamed of, or that you secretly fear God won't help you with. God yearns for you to let Him be all-powerful in your life. To do that, you must go beyond your fears, beyond your human flesh, and go beyond your comfort zone by seeking God with your whole being. He's waiting for you.

YOUR PROMISE TO GOD . . .

God, I open myself to You completely—the good, the bad, and the ugly. I trust that You will embrace me and cleanse me of my sins.

Healing

Bless the Lord, O my soul. And forget not all His benefits: who forgives you all your iniquities, who heals all your diseases, who redeems your life from destruction, who crowns you with lov- ingkindness and tender mercies, who satisfies your mouth with good things, so that your youth is renewed like the eagle's.

(Psalm 103:2–5)

You like the finer things, but do you know that the finest thing you have is your bond: with yourself, with your friends and family, and most importantly, with God. It's easy to get distracted by so-called problems in our lives, but looked at through the lens of our destiny on earth, they then are seen not as problems but as opportunities. Opportunities for what you might ask. Opportunities to draw closer to yourself, to connect more deeply with your community, and to become God's beloved lady. Our healing comes from our seeing our lives as opportunities to fulfill God's desires.

YOUR PROMISE TO GOD . . .

I will view my obstacles as opportunities, for even my problems will help me get closer to You.

Healing

Blessed are the poor in spirit, for theirs is the king-
dom of heaven.
Blessed are those who mourn, for they shall be
comforted.
Blessed are the meek, for they shall inherit the
earth.
Blessed are those who hunger and thirst for their
righteousness, for they shall be filled.
Blessed are the merciful, for they shall obtain
mercy.
Blessed are the pure in heart, for they shall see
God.

(Matthew 5:3–8)

Have you noticed that those who talk the talk rarely walk the walk? But those who live in God's principles every day are shining examples without having to say a word. To become the woman God would have you be, wear the crown of humbleness. Adorn yourself with humility and invest yourself in service. Become the Godly woman who can and will inspire others.

YOUR PROMISE TO GOD . . .

I will humbly walk the path You've laid before me, serving others and serving You.

Healing

Confess your trespasses to one another, and pray for one another, that you may be healed. The effective, fervent prayer of a righteous man avails much.

(James 5:16)

I am a firm believer in the power of prayer, because I have seen it work miracles in the lives of so many. There is nothing more powerful in the process of healing—spiritual, emotional, and physical—than prayer. Join with your friends and ask them to become a partner in prayer for you, and do the same for them. Become strong through prayer.

YOUR PROMISE TO GOD . . .

I will lift up my voice and ask for Your blessing.

Hopelessness

Hopelessness

Have faith in God, for assuredly I say to you, whoever says to this mountain "Be removed and be cast into the sea," and does not doubt in his heart, but believes that those things he says will be done, he will have whatever he says. Therefore I say to you, whatever things you ask when you pray, believe that you will receive them, and you will have them.

(Mark 11:22–24)

Hopelessness is like a cancer. It spreads throughout your soul, stealing your joy, killing your energy, and making you feel like there is no reason to go on. Hopelessness makes you weak—weak in body and weak in sprit. There is only one antidote to the cancer called hopelessness—and this is flooding your life with the Lord. Pray constantly, read the Bible, reach out to others in your church. God will take your weakness and make you strong. Your power is in God.

YOUR PROMISE TO GOD . . .

In my darkness, I will look to You, and You will be my light.

Hopelessness

If you love Me, keep My commandments. And I will pray the Father, and He will give you another Helper, that He may abide with you forever—the Spirit of truth, whom the world cannot receive, because it neither sees Him, nor knows Him; but you know Him, for He dwells with you and will be in you. I will not leave you orphans; I will come to you.

(John 14:15–18)

You feel alone. You feel like no one understands you, or will ever love you. You feel unseen, small, worthless. But the Lord has not only seen you, He made you from the first and loves you. He has a special purpose—just for you—that is vital to His plan. Rejoice now, for God is your Father and you do not take even one step by yourself.

When I feel alone, I will turn to You. You are ever faithful. You are always there.

Hopelessness

And the Scriptures were written to teach and encourage us by giving us hope.

(Romans 15:4[+])

We are constantly bombarded with bad news. From TV news to beauty-shop gossip, from negative songs on the radio to even good friends who will drag you down. It's so easy to let Satan sap your strength. But God is always Good News. When the bad news gets you down, God's powerful Word will lift you up. Trust Scripture and turn to it daily for support and strength. It will bring you hope.

YOUR PROMISE TO GOD . . .

I will read Your Word daily. It will be my guide and support.

Hopelessness

Do not let your heart envy sinners,
but be zealous for the fear of the Lord all the day;
for surely there is a hereafter,
and your hope will not be cut off.

(Proverbs 23:17–18)

It's easy to feel despair when you are focused on what others seem to have that you don't. God is not withholding pleasure and happiness from your life. Rather, He is preparing you for something even greater than what others appear to have. Don't fret! Don't envy! Have hope, for God has a plan for you and, sister, it's more than you could ever dream. Relax and let Him reveal it to you.

YOUR PROMISE TO GOD . . .

I will trust that You will give me more than I could ever imagine.

Hopelessness

These things I have spoken to you, that in Me you may have peace. In the world you will have tribulation; but be of good cheer, I have overcome the world.

(John 16:33)

Sometimes we get weary. Sometimes the weight of our little world makes us feel like we're carrying big bags of heavy stones around our hearts. We feel weighted down. But Jesus reminds us to keep focused on Him, to keep faithful to His Word. He has paid the price, and now is the time to turn away from our worldly problems and center our life on the peace that only Jesus can bring.

YOUR PROMISE TO GOD . . .

Instead of focusing on the world, I will focus on The One. Jesus brings me peace.

Hopelessness

For we are His workmanship, creating in Jesus Christ for good works, which God prepared beforehand that we should walk in them.

(Ephesians 2:10)

Do you realize that God had you in mind when He created the Universe? Yes, sister, you are a vital part of God's unfolding plan. So whenever you feel lonely or unloved, remember that right here and right now, you are exactly where you are supposed to be—and God will walk every step with you. Rejoice!

YOUR PROMISE TO GOD . . .

I will work steadily on my path, knowing that You set my course and that You walk beside me.

Happiness

Happiness

Don't worry about anything; instead, pray about everything. Tell God what you need, and thank him for all he has done. If you do this, you will experience God's peace, which is far more wonderful than the human mind can understand. His peace will guard your hearts and minds as you live in Christ Jesus.

(Philippians 4:6–7*)

You daydream about how good your life will be once your bills are paid, or once you find a man, or once you lose those extra pounds. But God wants you to be happy now, not later. In fact, once you realize the greatness and goodness of God, you can begin living in His joy right now. Despite the outer circumstances, you can choose God's inner peace.

YOUR PROMISE TO GOD . . .

I rejoice in Your greatness and goodness. You bring joy to my life.

Happiness

Those who listen to instruction will prosper; those who trust the Lord will be happy.

(*Proverbs 16:20**)

There are some women who believe that if they do "all the right things" they will be happy. If they attend every workshop, pray perfectly in front of others, never miss even one Sunday of church, then they will experience the joy of the Lord (not to mention the admiration of others). While those things are admirable and all great goals to work toward, true joy comes from the inspired Word of God. Only in God will you be happy.

YOUR PROMISE TO GOD . . .

True joy comes from having a personal relationship with You. I will live my life according to Your Word.

Happiness

How I rejoice in God my Savior!

(Luke 1:47)*

You think that the right house or the right man will make you happy—or the right weight, the right bank account, the right friends, the right job. Oh, how misguided is that kind of thinking. Happiness is an inside job, not based on what's going on around you. Choose happiness first; everything else will follow. Get right with God and you'll experience happiness previously unknown.

YOUR PROMISE TO GOD . . .

You are the source of all happiness. Praise to You, Lord Jesus Christ.

Happiness

So I saw that there is nothing better for people
than to be happy in their work. That is why they
are here! No one will bring them back from death
to enjoy life in the future.

(Ecclesiastes 3:22 *)

You might complain about your job, but have you ever stopped to consider that God has placed you exactly where you are for a reason? You are called to be a great ambassador of Christ in your workplace, even if you don't like where you work (perhaps especially if you don't like where you work). Develop the happiness that comes from excellence. Read your Bible before work. Choose to be happy. And then don't be surprised if someone at your job sees you smiling from inner joy and asks you why you are so happy. Tell them God loves them and spread the joy.

YOUR PROMISE TO GOD . . .

Instead of complaining at work, I will experience the joy of knowing that I am serving You.

Happiness

"Sing and rejoice, O daughter of Zion! For behold,
I am coming and I will dwell in your midst," says
the Lord.

(Zechariah 2:10)

Girl, I've got news for you. God did not create you to whine, moan, complain, gossip, or generally walk around like you are the world's biggest victim. No! God created you for His special purpose, and that includes living in joy. When was the last time you felt joy for the whole day? Don't let the devils steal your joy. Choose to feel good right now. If you need a reason to feel joy, try this: God loves you!

YOUR PROMISE TO GOD . . .

I'm not a victim; I'm a victor because I am my Father's daughter.

Happiness

Sin is no longer your master, for you are no longer subject to the law, which enslaves you to sin. Instead, you are free by God's grace.

(Romans 6:14*)

Making the decision for Christ means freeing yourself from all the lies, all the time and energy that you have put into everything that in the end tore you down and made you feel broken. Isn't it good to know that the Lord has every piece that has your name on it, and can not only put you back together, but will gladly remakes you anew in His image! Follow God's plan for your life, pray throughout the day, humble yourself before the Lord, and then watch the miracles He performs in your life. It's good to be free from the confinement of sin. Let freedom ring!

YOUR PROMISE TO GOD . . .

I will follow Your plan and open myself to the miracles You will bestow upon me.

Love

Love

Continue to love each other with true Christian love.

(Hebrews 13:1*)

I know you think he looks good, and he has all the right words, but does he love Christ? Or are you settling for a Mr. Right Now just because he's Mr. Right Here? You are a sensitive woman with a great capacity to love. It's also important to match your sensitivity and your love with your mind, so that you are not making a foolish choice. In other words, is he the right man for you? Here's a quick test to determine if he is: Does he love God with his whole heart and soul? Does he actively try to know God's will for his life? Is he a praying man? Do his actions align with his words? Is he trustworthy? Pray to the Lord for guidance, and don't say yes to any man just because you can. Wait for Mr. Right, because the Lord has someone special in mind for you. You don't want to be wasting time with someone else!

YOUR PROMISE TO GOD . . .

I will wait for the man who loves me and loves You.

Love

But if you are willing to listen, I say, love your enemies. Do good to those who hate you.

(Luke 6:27*)

It's easy to love those who love you first. It's infinitely harder to love those who do you wrong. Loving and forgiving often walk hand in hand, and sometimes the best way to forgive someone who has hurt you is to love them with the love of Christ within you. When you can bless those who have wounded you, when you can bless your past, then you are living in the love that the Lord intended for you. Love is the ingredient, the yeast, so to speak, that will help forgiveness grow. Forgiveness in turn fosters great love. In this way they work hand in hand and help to create healthy love in your life. Ask God for enough love to love and forgive those who hurt you, and also ask for wisdom so that you cannot be hurt again.

Your Promise to God . . .

I will take the love You fill me with and share it. I will forgive those who hurt me.

Love

I love those who love me, and those who seek me diligently will find me.

(Proverbs 8:17)

She may look like a mean coworker, but she has Christ inside of her. He might look like the man that just walked out on you, but he has Christ inside of him. Your mother may drive you crazy, but she has Christ inside, too. Whoever it is that is pushing your buttons, the way to respond is from love. Not from anger or pain or hurt, but from love. Take a deep breath on that one! It is only responding to people in our lives from love that will bring about healing. I'm not talking about unhealthy love where you give it all away to others, in whatever form, and then don't get anything back. That isn't love, that is low self-esteem. I'm talking about love that is from the overflow that you feel in your heart, the overflow from the love that Jesus gives you. There's always more love where that came from.

YOUR PROMISE TO GOD . . .

I will interact with everyone in my life with a heart full of love.

Love

If I could speak in any language in heaven or on earth but didn't love others, I would only be making meaningless noise like a loud gong or a clanging cymbal.

(I Corinthans 13:1*)

Speaking in the language of love is like learning a whole new language! Why? Because it requires your whole being. It requires you to respond verbally only after making sure that your response is in line with the love of Christ. It requires of you to respond from your heart, not your head, and certainly not your ego or your wound. It requires you to open yourself up rather than shut yourself down. Love does not need you to protect yourself, it only needs you to give it away generously and wisely. Women innately know a lot about love, but I've found that the one thing most women don't know about love is how much of it resides within them, for themselves and for other people. And especially for God. Seek to discover the love in yourself, and you'll be surprised just how much love you have.

YOUR PROMISE TO GOD . . .

Love resides within me and I will share it with an open heart.

Love

Do not love the world or the things in the world. If anyone loves the world, the love of the Father is not in him.

(1 John 2:15)

What do you value in your life? Look around your home and see the evidence of what you value. Is the TV more important than the Bible—which gets more of your time? Is talking on the phone more important than praying—who hears more from you, your friends or God? Are clothes and things more important than the anointment of the Spirit—are you shopping more than you are communing with other Christians? In other words, are you loving the world more than you are loving the Lord? Surround your outer world with what you value most in your inner world, and that is the Lord. Getting your love prioritized is important, because that new dress you covet won't be in fashion much longer, but a life with Christ can last for eternity.

YOUR PROMISE TO GOD . . .

I will put my love of God above all other loves.

Love

I have loved you even as the Father has loved me.
Remain in my love.

(John 15:9*)

When Jesus asks you to remain in His love, He is asking you to obey Him completely. Not some of the time, not only on those things that you like or that are easy, but in all areas. Now, I know that may seem hard to do, but the good news is that your first step is just to be willing. Be willing to ask for His help. Pray, sing a hymn, sit in quiet, take a walk and talk with the Lord—do anything that illustrates your willingness to the Lord, and do it as often as you can. Your willingness turns into His opportunity to use you for His loving purpose on this earth. It is truly amazing to realize that you were loved by God even before you were born, because God knew you and wanted you from the start. That kind of complete and unconditional love is beautiful and exciting. Thank the Lord for loving you more than life itself.

YOUR PROMISE TO GOD . . .

I will remain in Your love and obey You completely.

Relationships

Relationships

Can two people walk together without agreeing on the direction?

(Amos 3:3*)

Do you need to have it your way, or no way? How can you have a healthy relationship when you want to call all the shots? Listen to me—it is vital that you are clear about one very important ingredient in a relationship: both of you must be focused on the Lord first in order to make it work. Agree to make the Lord your destination and you'll find you are walking in the same direction.

YOUR PROMISE TO GOD . . .

Jesus, you are the foundation of every healthy relationship. I will keep You at the center of my life.

Relationships

All flesh is as grass,
and all the glory of man as the flower of grass.
The grass withers,
and its flower falls away,
but the word of the Lord endures forever.

(1 Peter 1:24–25)

You wait by the phone for his call, wishing and hoping he'll dial your number. You wonder if you should call first, or call again, or email him. Perhaps drop by to visit him, or spend hours talking about him to your friends. Do you see how much time you spend thinking about him? Let me ask you a question—how much time do you spend thinking about Jesus? Why don't you call Him up in your heart, visit Him in your church, and talk about Him to your friends? He's waiting, and a relationship with Him will last forever.

YOUR PROMISE TO GOD . . .

Lord, you are ever faithful to me, and I will be faithful to You.

Relationships

What I meant was that you are not to associate
with anyone who clams to be a Christian yet in-
dulges in sexual sin, or is greedy, or worships
idols, or is abusive, or a drunkard, or a swindler.
Don't even eat with such people.

(I Corinthians 5:11*)

Sometimes the man you most want to date is the man you know in your heart isn't right for you. The temptation is strong, and you tell yourself that he is just going through a phase, or that you can compromise for him because you can change him later. Don't believe the lies, whether they are the ones he is telling you or the ones you are telling yourself. Look at his actions, look at his behavior, and make the decision that God would have you make. The Lord is clear about such things, and has given you these guidelines in His Word—not to cause you pain but rather to save you from pain! God is on your side, and understand that every page of the Bible is a guidebook to help you to be His Lady.

YOUR PROMISE TO GOD . . .

I know You want the best for me. I will look to You to guide me in all my relationships.

Relationships

So encourage each other and build each other up,
just as you are already doing.
(1 Thessalonians 5:11*)

I know how easy it is to talk trash about someone. I know you know how hurtful it is when someone talks trash about you. And I know you know how God wants you to behave. When you tear down others, you tear down yourself, and even worse, you defile the Lord. When you act in love and encouragement toward others, you are not only lifting up them and yourself, you are being a powerful witness for God. Nothing brings two people together—be it you and a man, a friend, or a family member—than kind words and even kinder action.

YOUR PROMISE TO GOD . . .

All of my words and actions will come from compassion.

Relationships

There are six things the Lord hates—no seven
   things he detests:
haughty eyes,
a lying tongue,
hands that kill the innocent,
a heart that plots evil,
feet that race to do wrong,
a false witness who pours out lies,
a person who sows discord among brothers.

(Proverbs 6:16–19*)

The Lord doesn't make rules to punish us or limit us. He doesn't want us to get hurt, so he gave us clear instructions on how to have strong, positive, life-enhancing relationships with others, with ourselves, and with God. Listen, study, and live by what He has to say to you. You will be a happier, more joyful daughter of God if you do.

YOUR PROMISE TO GOD . . .

I want to be a better friend, daughter, sister, mother—just a better person. Your Word tells me what I need to do and I will endeavor to be the kind of person You want me to be.

Relationships

Do not withhold good from those who deserve it when it's in your power to help them. If you can help your neighbor now, don't say, "Come back tomorrow, and then I'll help you."

(Proverbs 3:27–28*)

I know you are busy with your job and your friends and your hobbies. But are you too busy for someone in need? People all around you are hurting—and they need your help right now. And if you are hurting, the best way to get through the hurt can sometimes be by helping others.

YOUR PROMISE TO GOD . . .

I will help those in need—to serve others, heal myself, and most of all, to serve You, my Lord.

Purpose

Purpose

So you should not be like cowering, fearful slaves.
You should behave instead like God's very own
children . . . calling him "Father, dear Father."

(*Romans 8:15**)

God does not want to be a distant relative in your life. God wants to be your dear Father, the one who you turn to constantly for strength. With God in your corner, there is no one who can defeat you. And yet, you sometimes have a defeatist attitude. Sister, lose that prison of defeat and wear the victory robe of God! Praise God, because the battle has already been won. Do you know the quickest way to change your life for the better? Praise. Praise God for everything you have, rather than everything you don't. Praise God for his eagerness to be your dear Father. Praise God that you have the choice to choose him now, above everything else. Praise God that he is the Creator, and that with him you are no longer a prisoner of the devil. Thank you, Jesus!

YOUR PROMISE TO GOD . . .

God, I turn to You and praise You because I know You're always there for me.

Purpose

The unmarried woman cares about the things of the Lord, that she may be holy both in body and in spirit.

(I Corinthians 7:34b)

Sometimes a woman will say to me, "I don't know what God wants from me." But God's Word is very clear: obey God in body and soul. Period. End of discussion. Surrendering to God's glorious Word is like reading a handbook on how to be a lady . . . His lady.

YOUR PROMISE TO GOD . . .

You have given me an instruction manual for how to lead my life—the Bible. I will read it, live it, and praise You for Your glory.

Purpose

For I can do everything with the help of Christ
who gives me the strength I need.

(Philippians 4:13*)

Do you feel like you could do just about anything if you only could figure out what you are supposed to do? Do you yearn for guidance? Wouldn't it be great if life came with an instruction manual? It does! It's called the Bible, and it plainly and clearly states our purpose, which is to be God's hands on this earth. Pray to the Lord, who is closer to you than even your breath, and He will help reveal to you His plan for you. Scour the Word of God and you will begin to see a map for you to follow. Praise God aloud, and often, and begin to see every moment as a new adventure in which to fulfill His plan. God wants you to succeed, and if you are willing to step up to the plate, you will not fail.

YOUR PROMISE TO GOD . . .

I will read Your Word and follow the plan that You have set before me.

Purpose

Well then, if we emphasize faith, does this mean that we can forget about the law? Of course not! In fact, only when we have faith do we truly fulfill the law.

(Romans 3:31*)

I know a woman who prayed to Jesus, asking for something that she wanted, and then she sat back and waited for Him to bring it right to her. She waited and waited and waited. She was so disappointed when nothing happened. She cried out, "Why is this happening to me? Why did the Lord forsake me?" The real question, though is this: Why did she forsake the Lord? Why did she give up the faith? What did the waiting mean for her? The Lord is working according to His timing, not yours. And there are times when you are going to be called upon to take responsibility and action before God can answer your prayer. A better prayer is this: *Dear God, please show me Your will. My joy comes from You, and so I ask that You show me how I can bring You joy. I am willing to serve You wholeheartedly. Use me, Lord. Thank you for everything. Amen.* Try this prayer, and see what happens!

YOUR PROMISE TO GOD . . .

I will pray for Your guidance and follow Your counsel.

Purpose

A wise woman builds her house; a foolish woman tears hers down with her own hands.

(Proverbs 14:1*)

Does it ever feel like you are your own worst enemy? Sometimes you might find yourself doing really well, and then all of a sudden you do or say something that completely takes away your treasure. You sabatoge yourself in thought, word, or action, and destroy what took you precious time to build. A wise woman knows that she must rely upon the Lord in order to create a base strong enough to withstand any storm, including those storms she creates herself. If you find that at times you are your own worst enemy, know that Jesus is your own best friend. He wants to introduce you to someone very special, someone who is going to help you become the lady He wants you to be—and that person is YOU! Let Him reveal to you His plans and vision for your life. He promises that His vision of you is more glorious than any vision you have for yourself.

YOUR PROMISE TO GOD . . .

I want to be the woman You created me to be. I will look to You to show me the way.

Purpose

You must accept whatever situation the Lord has put you in, and continue on as you were when God first called you.

(1 Corinthians 7:17*)

God has placed you exactly where He wants you. He has called you to where you are for a reason. You are His emissary, His voice and hands on this earth. When you learn God's word and pray for His guidance, He can use you for His purpose, beginning with yourself and the people around you.

YOUR PROMISE TO GOD . . .

I am here for a reason—to fulfill Your purpose for me. I will walk the path You have laid before me and I will serve You faithfully.

Abundance

Abundance

For you have need of endurance, so that after you have done the will of God, you may receive the promise.

(Hebrews 10:36)

We usually want what we want when we want it. Am I right? But where is God in that equation? God has great treasures—physical and spiritual treasures—in store for us. All we are asked to do is obey God's Word and wait on the Lord. So hurry and wait for God to bless you!

YOUR PROMISE TO GOD . . .

I do believe in You and know that You will bless me.
I will wait humbly for Your time.

Abundance

Remember, it is a message to obey, not just to listen to. If you don't obey, you are only fooling yourself. But if you keep looking steadily into God's perfect law—the law that sets you free—and if you do what it says and don't forget what you heard, then God will bless you for doing it.

(James 1:22, 25*)

God promises to bless us—but first we must be faithful servants of His word. By praying, tithing, and reading the Bible daily, we develop the spiritual muscle with which to receive God's goodness. We also begin to understand that true abundance is greater than just dollars and cents. It is the peace and love and joy of our Lord in our hearts.

YOUR PROMISE TO GOD . . .

God, I promise to serve you faithfully. With You in my life, I am rich beyond compare.

Abundance

"Bring all the tithes into the storehouse, that there may be food in My house, and try Me now in this," says the Lord of hosts, "if I will not open for you the windows of heaven and pour out for you such a blessing that there will not be room enough to receive it."

(Malachi 3:10)

Don't be like so many who want all of the good without any of the responsibility. They want God to somehow magically bestow upon them whatever they want. And they want it right now! The Lord, however, cannot give anything to people who refuse to give to God first. When you tithe—that is, give back of your time and finances to where you are spiritually fed—you become an open vessel that the Lord can fill. Become the greatest giver, and God will also make you a great receiver.

Your Promise to God . . .

Lord, I know that everything I have is Yours, because all I have You have given me. I give back to You to thank You for this bounty.

Abundance

But this I say: He who sows sparingly will also reap sparingly, and he who sows bountifully will also reap bountifully. So let each one give as he purposes in his heart, not grudgingly or of necessity; for God loves a cheerful giver. And God is able to make all grace abound toward you, that you, always having all sufficiency in all things, may have an abundance for every good work.

(II Corinthians 9:6–8)

If you reread the Bible verse on the previous page, you will notice an equation. Reaping comes after sowing—and sowing means giving. But Jesus goes on to say that it is not enough to just give; rather, we must give with gratitude. How is your reaping these days? If it isn't where you believe the Lord would have it, practice grateful giving and begin it today.

YOUR PROMISE TO GOD . . .

I always feel full of love when I do Your good work. I know that reaping is a result of sowing, but knowing that I am making You happy is reward enough.

Abundance

Give your burdens to the Lord and he will take care of you.

(Psalm 55:22a*)

God is not some distant CEO in the sky that takes weeks or months just to schedule an appointment with you to talk. God is available right now, right where you are—and He wants to hear from you. What are you waiting for? Pour out your heart to Him, be "real" with Him. Starting a dialogue with the Lord is one of the first steps to receiving your blessings. It's such a gift to know that He hears us and wants only the best for us.

YOUR PROMISE TO GOD . . .

God, I know You are here for me and hear all my prayers. Can we talk?

Abundance

Always remember that it is the Lord your God who give's you power to become rich, and he does it to fulfill the covenant he made with your ancestors.

(Deuteronomy 8:18*)

God is the Creator. Life itself comes from God Almighty. Just as God breathed life into Adam, He wants to breathe life into you and your experience on earth. What is standing in His way? You are! Step aside, and let God be God in your life. The result will be that God will fulfill His promise of blessing His faithful. And you will live as a true daughter of Zion!

Your Promise to God . . .

Lord, I know that You want to bestow upon me all the greatest treasures in the world. I open my heart to You and accept them.

Promise Pages

Promise from God

Lord, although I am feeling bad right now, I know that You have promised me . . .

_____

_____

_____

_____

_____

_____

_____

_____

_____

_____

_____

_____

_____

and You always fulfill Your promises!

Promise to God

You give me everything I need, and only ask in return that I am faithful to You. Lord, I promise You I will . . .

_____

_____

_____

_____

_____

_____

_____

_____

_____

_____

_____

_____

_____

_____

and I will strive to be Your faithful servant.

Promise from God

Lord, although I am feeling bad right now, I know that You have promised me . . .

_____

_____

_____

_____

_____

_____

_____

_____

_____

_____

_____

_____

_____

and You always fulfill Your promises!

Promise to God

You give me everything I need, and only ask in return that I am faithful to You. Lord, I promise You I will . . .

_____

_____

_____

_____

_____

_____

_____

_____

_____

_____

_____

_____

_____

and I will strive to be Your faithful servant.

Promise from God

Lord, although I am feeling bad right now, I know that You have promised me . . .

_____

_____

_____

_____

_____

_____

_____

_____

_____

_____

_____

_____

_____

_____

_____

and You always fulfill Your promises!

Promise to God

You give me everything I need, and only ask in return that I am faithful to You. Lord, I promise You I will . . .

_____

_____

_____

_____

_____

_____

_____

_____

_____

_____

_____

_____

_____

_____

and I will strive to be Your faithful servant.

Promise from God

Lord, although I am feeling bad right now, I know that You have promised me . . .

_____

_____

_____

_____

_____

_____

_____

_____

_____

_____

_____

_____

_____

_____

and You always fulfill Your promises!

Promise to God

You give me everything I need, and only ask in return that I am faithful to You. Lord, I promise You I will . . .

and I will strive to be Your faithful servant.

Promise from God

Lord, although I am feeling bad right now, I know that You have promised me . . .

_____

_____

_____

_____

_____

_____

_____

_____

_____

_____

_____

_____

_____

_____

and You always fulfill Your promises!

Promise to God

You give me everything I need, and only ask in return that I am faithful to You. Lord, I promise You I will . . .

_____

_____

_____

_____

_____

_____

_____

_____

_____

_____

_____

_____

_____

and I will strive to be Your faithful servant.

Promise from God

Lord, although I am feeling bad right now, I know that You have promised me . . .

_____

_____

_____

_____

_____

_____

_____

_____

_____

_____

_____

_____

_____

and You always fulfill Your promises!

Promise to God

You give me everything I need, and only ask in return that I am faithful to You. Lord, I promise You I will . . .

_____

_____

_____

_____

_____

_____

_____

_____

_____

_____

_____

_____

_____

and I will strive to be Your faithful servant.

Promise from God

Lord, although I am feeling bad right now, I know that You have promised me . . .

_____

_____

_____

_____

_____

_____

_____

_____

_____

_____

_____

_____

_____

and You always fulfill Your promises!

Promise to God

You give me everything I need, and only ask in return that I am faithful to You. Lord, I promise You I will . . .

_____

_____

_____

_____

_____

_____

_____

_____

_____

_____

_____

_____

_____

_____

and I will strive to be Your faithful servant.

Promise from God

Lord, although I am feeling bad right now, I know that You have promised me . . .

---

and You always fulfill Your promises!

Promise to God

You give me everything I need, and only ask in return that I am faithful to You. Lord, I promise You I will . . .

_____

_____

_____

_____

_____

_____

_____

_____

_____

_____

_____

_____

_____

and I will strive to be Your faithful servant.

Promise from God

Lord, although I am feeling bad right now, I know that You have promised me . . .

_____

_____

_____

_____

_____

_____

_____

_____

_____

_____

_____

_____

_____

and You always fulfill Your promises!

Promise to God

You give me everything I need, and only ask in return that I am faithful to You. Lord, I promise You I will . . .

_____

_____

_____

_____

_____

_____

_____

_____

_____

_____

_____

_____

_____

_____

and I will strive to be Your faithful servant.

Promise from God

Lord, although I am feeling bad right now, I know that You have promised me . . .

_____

_____

_____

_____

_____

_____

_____

_____

_____

_____

_____

_____

_____

and You always fulfill Your promises!

Promise to God

You give me everything I need, and only ask in return that I am faithful to You. Lord, I promise You I will . . .

_____

_____

_____

_____

_____

_____

_____

_____

_____

_____

_____

_____

_____

and I will strive to be Your faithful servant.

Promise from God

Lord, although I am feeling bad right now, I know that You have promised me . . .

_____

_____

_____

_____

_____

_____

_____

_____

_____

_____

_____

_____

_____

_____

and You always fulfill Your promises!

Promise to God

You give me everything I need, and only ask in return that I am faithful to You. Lord, I promise You I will . . .

and I will strive to be Your faithful servant.